FISH

FISH

MICHAEL GEORGE

THE CHILD'S WORLD

DESIGN
Bill Foster of Albarella & Associates, Inc.

PHOTO CREDITS
Marty Snyderman: front cover, 9, 13, 13 (inset), 19, 25, 29
Norbert Wu: back cover, 2, 11, 15, 27, 31
COMSTOCK/Russ Kinne: 17, 23
COMSTOCK/Phylis Greenberg: 21

Distributed to schools and libraries
in the United States by
ENCYCLOPAEDIA BRITANNICA EDUCATIONAL CORP
310 South Michigan Ave.
Chicago, Illinois 60604

Library of Congress Cataloging-in-Publication Data
George, Michael, 1964-
Fish/Michael George.
p. cm. — (Child's World Wildlife Library)
Summary: Describes the characteristics and behavior of
such fish as the hammerhead shark, piranha, and porcupine fish.
ISBN 0-89565-701-5
1. Fishes — Juvenile literature.   [1. Fishes.]   I. Title.
II. Series.   91-13376
QL617.2.G46   1991   CIP
597—dc20   AC

CONTENTS

The earth is inhabited by millions of living creatures. Being land animals ourselves, people are most familiar with animals that live on the land. However, most of our planet is covered by water. Beneath the earth's rivers, lakes, and oceans is a world inhabited by strange and fascinating creatures.

Fish are among the most common animals of the underwater world. There are more than 30,000 different kinds of fish. They can be found in cold polar seas and in warm coral reefs, from rushing mountain streams to thick, murky swamplands.

Although all fish live in water, each kind of fish has adapted to its particular surroundings and way of life. As a result, fish differ greatly in their appearance and behavior. Fish come in all sorts of shapes, sizes, and colors. Some are shy and timid, while others are fierce and dangerous. Most fish spend their entire lives in water. However, some fish can travel across dry land and others can even fly. The following are some of the fascinating fish that inhabit the earth.

HAMMERHEAD SHARK

The hammerhead shark is one of the most common sharks in the world. Hammerheads live off coastlines and coral reefs in warm, tropical oceans. Adults grow up to 15 feet long and many weigh over 1,000 pounds. The hammerhead's most distinctive feature is its large, bar-shaped head. The fish's eyes and nostrils are located at the tips of its odd-looking head. Like many other sharks, the hammerhead has a large, powerful jaw that contains five or six rows of teeth. Though they normally feed on other fish, hammerheads have been known to attack humans.

PIRANHA

Piranhas swim in the dark, murky rivers of South America. Although they grow only about 12 inches long, piranhas are among the most vicious fish in the world. A single bite from a piranha can be painful, but it is not likely to be fatal. However, once a victim has been bitten, the fresh blood attracts hundreds of other piranhas. Thrashing wildly, the fish tear at the animal's flesh with their razor-sharp teeth. Within minutes, piranhas can strip their victim's body clean, leaving only a skeleton behind.

PORCUPINE FISH

Like all living creatures, fish have developed many methods for defending themselves from enemies. Among the most interesting defenses is the one perfected by the porcupine fish. This unusual creature inhabits coral reefs in warm, tropical seas. Growing only two feet long, the porcupine fish looks like a tasty snack to larger enemies. When a hungry enemy approaches, however, the porcupine fish gulps water with all its might. It quickly inflates into a swollen, spiny balloon. The fish's sharp spines are enough to scare away even the hungriest enemy.

SAILFISH

The sailfish is one of the most magnificent of all ocean creatures. Adult sailfish grow up to 12 feet long and may weigh over 100 pounds. The fish is named for its enormous dorsal fin, which stands up like a sail above the fish's sleek, tapered body. The sailfish is one of the fastest fish in the world, able to swim at speeds up to 60 miles per hour. Because of its size, speed, and beauty, the sailfish is a highly prized game fish. After hooking a sailfish, a person may struggle for hours to bring the fighting, leaping fish to the boat.

FLYING HATCHET FISH

The flying hatchet fish lives in the rivers of tropical South America. Growing only three inches long, the tiny animal looks like an appetizing meal to many larger fish. However, the flying hatchet fish is not an easy meal to catch. When threatened by an enemy, the tiny creature races toward the water's surface. With a sudden burst of speed, the fish blasts out of the water and soars into the air. Beating its fins as though they are wings, the flying hatchet fish can remain in the air for up to 60 feet. By the time it lands, the fish is well out of range of its confused enemy.

MORAY EEL

The moray eel is a unique, snakelike fish that inhabits coral reefs. Armed with a gaping mouth filled with sharp, pointed teeth, the moray eel is a vicious-looking creature. Like a storybook monster, the fish hides in dark, underwater caves. When an appetizing meal swims by, the eel lunges from its hiding place and seizes the unsuspecting victim. Though they feed primarily on other fish, moray eels will attack a person if a foot or a hand comes within range. Once in the grasp of the moray's powerful jaws, it is almost impossible to escape.

MUDSKIPPER

Mudskippers are known for their comical appearance and their unfishlike behavior. They live along tropical coastlines in the shallow waters of swamps and tidal mud flats. The mudskipper's front fins are strong and powerful, enabling it to travel across the most unlikely terrain — dry land. The mudskipper escapes its aquatic enemies by hopping across the mud flats like a clumsy grasshopper. The fish also hunts for its favorite foods — worms, beetles, and flies — outside of its watery home.

CATFISH

Among the millions of creatures that inhabit the earth, few are as ugly as the catfish. Catfish can be easily recognized by the long, whiskerlike barbels that hang from their chins and gills. These barbels act as feelers, helping the catfish swim and find food on the murky bottoms of lakes and rivers. Although the barbels are harmless, catfish have sharp, dangerous spines on their fins. Unlike most other fish, catfish do not have scales. Their bodies are smooth and slimy. Despite their disgusting appearance, catfish are considered a delicacy throughout the world.

STINGRAY

The stingray is a unique, flattened fish that often lies hidden on sandy sea bottoms. The stingray's eyes are on the upperside of its body, always alert for a passing meal. When an appetizing meal swims by, the stingray flops down and smothers its victim. The stingray's mouth is located on the underside of its body. It is filled with tough, flattened teeth that can crush crabs, clams, and other hard-shelled animals. Although the stingray is a timid fish, it is not defenseless. The stingray's whiplike tail has a long, poisonous spine that can seriously injure an enemy.

OARFISH

The oarfish has been the subject of terrifying sea stories for thousands of years. This legendary fish lives in the dark depths of the oceans. Resembling a mythical sea serpent, some oarfish grow 30 feet long and weigh up to 600 pounds. The fish's dorsal fin stands above its head and neck like a magnificent crown. The oarfish gets its name from two slender, oarlike fins that dangle below its chin. These fins probably act as touch organs. They help the oarfish find food as it slithers through the murky waters of the ocean bottom.

SEA DRAGON

Sea dragons live in the shallow waters off the coast of Australia. They have long, leaflike growths and spines covering much of their bodies. The strange decorations help sea dragons hide among underwater seaweed, algae, and grass. The sea dragon's long snout is used like a vacuum cleaner to suck up immature sea animals. Unlike most other animals, young sea dragons develop in a pouch on the male. When they leave their father's pouch, the baby sea dragons are only the size of a fly. As they mature, some sea dragons grow 12 inches long.

DEEP-SEA ANGLERFISH

The deep-sea anglerfish lives in the dark, murky depths of the ocean. Male anglerfish grow only six inches long and spend most of their lives attached to a female. Female anglerfish, on the other hand, grow up to five feet long. They lurk among rocks and seaweed on the ocean bottom. Special cells, called *photosphores*, make the tip of the female's dorsal fin shine. The fish dangles this glowing bait in front of her huge, gaping mouth. When a smaller fish comes too close, the deep-sea anglerfish gobbles it up.

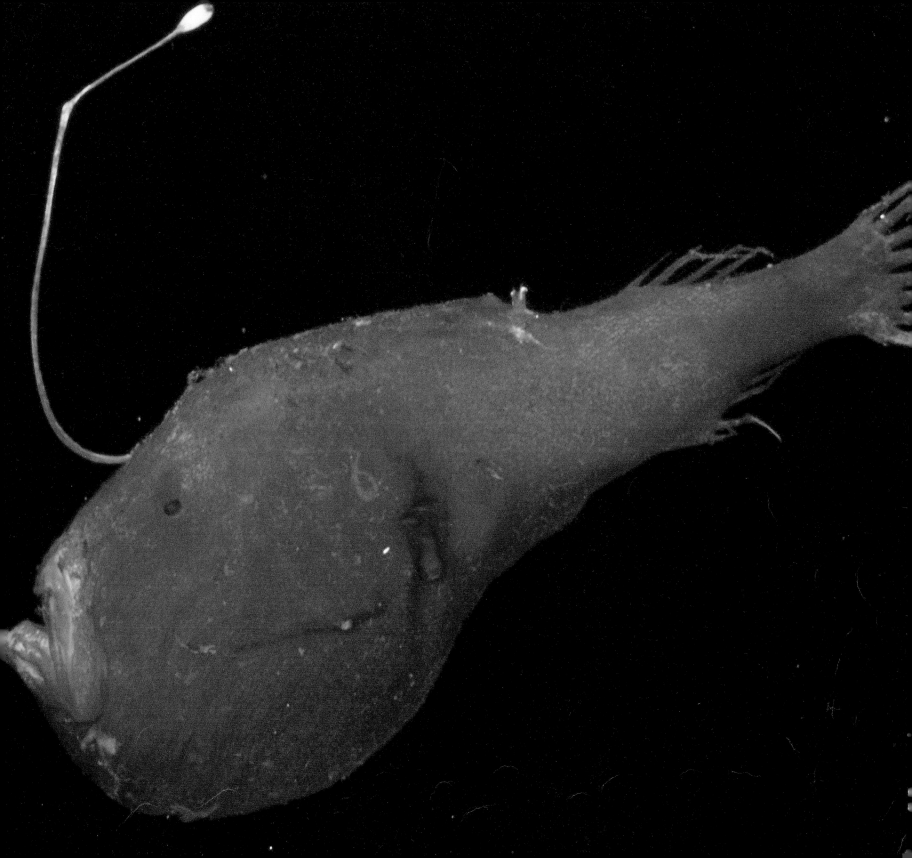